THE MARY A. McBRIDE-LEE STORY

A Child's View from the Foot of the Edmund Pettus Bridge

MARY A. McBRIDE-LEE

THE MARY A. McBRIDE-LEE STORY
A Child's View from the Foot of the
Edmund Pettus Bridge

Copyright ©2025 Mary A. McBride-Lee

All rights reserved. No part of this book may be reproduced or transmitted in any form or by any means electronic or mechanical. Including photocopying, recording or by any information storage and retrieval system, without written permission from Mary A. McBride-Lee or HOV Publishing.

Published by HOV Publishing,
a division of HOV, LLC.
Bridgeport, CT

Illustrator: HOV Publishing Design Team

For More Information, Contact:
Rev. Mary A. McBride-Lee
Tel: 203-767-9776
mlee@bridgeportedu.net

ISBN: 978-1-955107-03-7 (hardcase)

Printed in the United States of America

This book is dedicated to

My mom Mary Bell Dale McBride, Marilyn Wagner Neice.
All the unsung heroes and Chiquita Stevenson.

There were so many of us, Mama said
we filled the house with love and noise.
I was the baby, number thirteen.
And I had a twin sister, Mattie.
We always shared a bed, a plate, and
sometimes...
even our shoes!

Our house was full of rules and hugs. Mama said, "Charity starts at home and spread abroad," Daddy said, "Education is your way out." So every morning, we got up, washed up, and lined up for school.

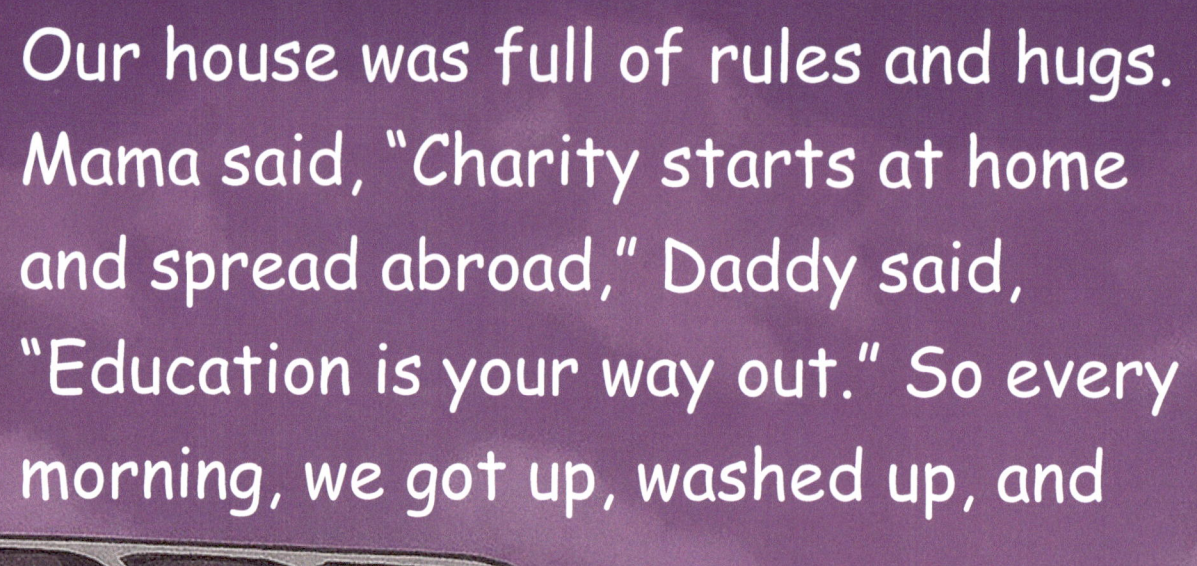

But there was no yellow bus for us.

We walked five miles. Every day. Across red dirt roads and muddy fields. Sometimes barefoot. Sometimes in hand-me-down shoes.

Our school was a one-room shack behind the church. No lunchroom. No lights. But we had pencils, books, and a teacher who believed in us. I sat with Mattie. She always let me answer first.

11

Every day, the big yellow bus rolled by.
The white children rode inside.
Some of them pointed.
Some of them laughed.
Sometimes they threw things
from the window.

I looked at the ground. But Mattie squeezed my hand.

"Keep walking," she whispered. "We've got learning to do."

So we did.

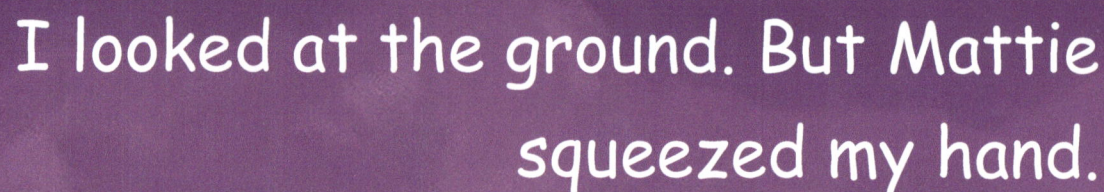

One day, Mama said,
"They're building a new school... for us!"

It had real windows.
Classrooms for every grade.
Grades 1 through 12, right in
Pine Apple, Alabama!

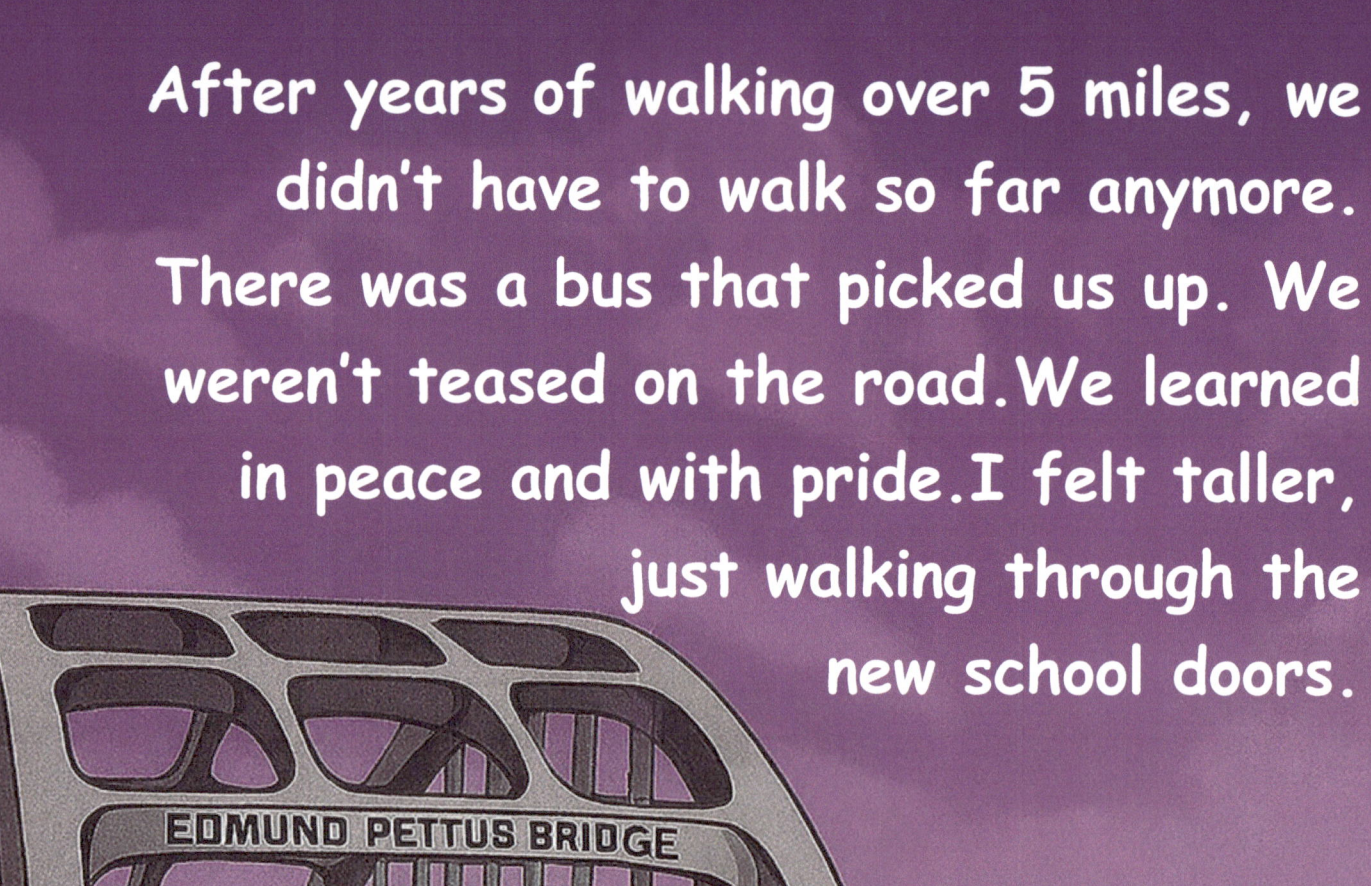

After years of walking over 5 miles, we didn't have to walk so far anymore. There was a bus that picked us up. We weren't teased on the road. We learned in peace and with pride. I felt taller, just walking through the new school doors.

But not everything stayed the same. As I got older, I saw things that weren't fair. Some families couldn't vote. Some couldn't speak up. I wanted to help. Quietly.

By the time I was sixteen, I had a secret. I went to meetings at Browns Temple with the late John Lewis and Dr. Martin Luther King Jr. as the speakers, hid flyers in my books, and listened.

I didn't tell Mama or Mattie.
Not because I didn't trust them, but
to keep them safe. I was careful.
Careful with my steps.
Careful with my words.
But inside, my heart
marched ahead.

And then came the
Edmund Pettus Bridge in 1965
in Selma, Alabama. The moment
that changed everything.
But that's another story...

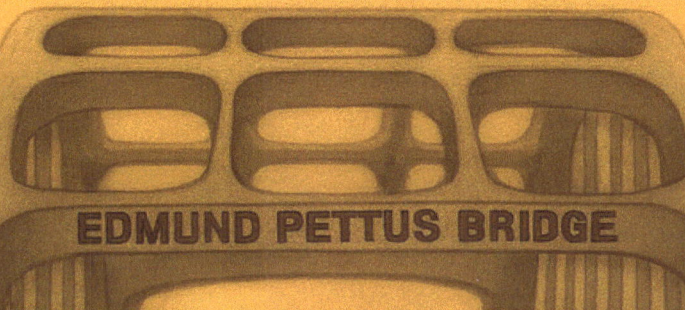

THE MARY A. McBRIDE-LEE STORY
ACTIVITY SECTION

SYMBOL KEY
THE STORY BEHIND THE BACKGROUND

Each symbol in Mary's world carries meaning. These images appear softly in the background for her story, reminding us of the courage, hope, and purpose behind every step toward justice.

SYMBOL	MEANING	WHAT IT REPRESENTS IN MARY'S STORY
Scales of Justice	Fairness and equality under the law	The dream of a world where every voice is heard and every right protected.
Raised Fist	Strength, unity, and resistance	The power of standing together, even when the world says "no."
Warning Triangle	Danger and awareness	The courage it takes to march forward, even when the path is unsafe.
Growing Plant	Freedom and democracy	The promise of America living up to its ideals *for all people*.
Eternal Flame	Hope and *new beginnings*	The seeds of change Mary and others helped to plant for future generations.

Can you be brave like Mary?

☐ I will stand up for someone being left out.

☐ I will use kind words.

☐ I will learn about my history.

☐ I will listen when someone shares their story.

*"You're never too small
to stand for something big."
– Rev. Mary McBride-Lee*

Did You Know?

♦ Brown Chapel A.M.E. Church is a real place in Selma, Alabama. It was one of the starting points for the famous civil rights marches in 1965.

♦ Dr. Martin Luther King Jr. was a pastor who believed in peaceful protest. He gave speeches, led marches, and helped people come together for change.

♦ John Lewis was only 25 years old when he led the march across the Edmund Pettus Bridge. He was very brave and became a congressman later in life.

♦ The Edmund Pettus Bridge is now a symbol of hope and courage. Every year, people walk across it to remember the marchers.

♦ Rev. Mary A. McBride-Lee was a young girl during the time of the Selma marches. She listened, learned, and became a leader in her own way.

Glossary

March – When a group of people walk together peacefully to show they care about a big problem and want things to change.

Chapel – A small church where people pray, sing, and meet to make plans.

Civil Rights – The rights that all people have to be treated fairly, no matter their skin color, where they live, or how they look.

Bridge – A structure that helps people cross over water or roads. The Edmund Pettus Bridge is a very important bridge in history.

Brave – Doing something even when it feels scary, because you know it's right.

Vote – To make a choice in an election. Grownups vote to help choose leaders and make laws.

Freedom – The power to do what is fair and right, without being told you can't because of who you are.

Leader – Someone who helps others, makes good choices, and stands up for what's right.

Pastor Mary Annette McBride-Lee

Born in Oakhill, Alabama, Pastor Mary Annette McBride-Lee is the youngest of thirteen children and a proud twin. A lifelong educator, she served in the Bridgeport Public School system for over 35 years and has represented her community as Councilwoman for Bridgeport's 135th District for 12 years.

Her early commitment to justice began in Selma, Alabama, where she marched alongside John Lewis, Hosea Williams, and Dr. Martin Luther King Jr. on "Bloody Sunday." In honor of her courage and activism, she received President Barack Obama's Civil Rights Foot Soldier Award, presented by Senator Richard Blumenthal.

Pastor McBride-Lee is the Founder and Senior Pastor of El-Shaddai Pentecostal Church in Bridgeport and the Founder of Project C.O.N.T.A.C.T., a youth outreach ministry. She also serves as a Fire Commissioner and member of the Democratic Town Committee.

She is the author of *At the Foot of the Edmund Pettus Bridge on Bloody Sunday* and the children's book *The Mary McBride-Lee Story: A Child's View from the Foot of the Edmund Pettus Bridge.*

Her life's work continues to inspire others to love, learn, and lead in faith and purpose.

www.ingramcontent.com/pod-product-compliance
Lightning Source LLC
Chambersburg PA
CBHW041411010526
44107CB00015B/1141